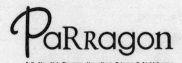

Adapted by Laurie McElroy

Based on the television series *Hannah Montana*, created by Michael Poryes and Rich Correll and Barry O'Brien

Part One is based on the episode written by Kim Friese

Part Two is based on the episode written by Kim Friese

PaRragon

Bath · New York · Singapore · Hong Kong · Cologne · Delhi · Melbourne

First published by Parragon in 2007
Parragon
Queen Street House
4 Queen Street
Bath BA1 1HE, UK

ISBN 978-1-4075-0239-7

Printed in UK

PART ONE

Chapter One

Miley Stewart ran down the stairs and into the kitchen, too excited to notice that her father was cleaning a huge fish. Her brother, Jackson, looked on, trying not to notice that his dinner had eyes.

"Dad, I know I have midterms on Monday, but the new Ashton Kutcher movie is previewing tonight!" Miley gazed at him with her absolutely sweetest smile. "How many 'pretty's do I need to put before 'please' for you to let me go?" she asked.

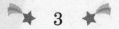

"Now, Mile - " Mr Stewart said, heading for the refrigerator.

That sounded like the beginning of a no. Miley cut him off. She ducked under his arm and stood between him and the lemons. "Pretty, pretty, pretty, pretty, pretty, pretty please, Dad. Please?"

"Whoa!" Mr Stewart held up his hands in what looked like surrender.

"I can go?" Miley asked excitedly.

"No, you can stop," Mr Stewart said. "You know you've got to study."

Miley wasn't about to give up. It *was* Ashton Kutcher, after all. "Yes, Dad, but if you think about it, midterms are halfway to finals, so I only need to study about half as hard," she argued. "And since I already study twice as hard as everybody else, I only need to study a quarter. So I've finished. See how that works?"

It was all perfectly logical to Miley, but her father didn't understand. "No. And you know what? I'm the dad and you lose. See how *that* works?" he asked.

Miley's shoulders slumped. Her two best friends, Lilly and Oliver, were going to the movie preview. So was everybody else. Everybody except Miley. She had to think of a way to get her dad to say yes.

Jackson saw a perfect opportunity to win some points with their dad. "You see, little sister, Dad, as a single parent, is only trying to make sure that you have the proper guidance. And I for one commend him on his commitment to education." He walked over with a big, fake smile on his face and patted Mr Stewart on the back.

Mr Stewart didn't buy *that*, either. "Son, I'm glad you feel that way. Because I'm committing you to staying home and

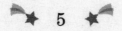

studying this weekend, too." He patted Jackson on the back and gave him an equally fake smile.

Jackson couldn't believe it. His plan had totally backfired.

"Ha-ha," Miley sang.

"But my midterms were last week," Jackson protested.

"I know," Mr Stewart said. "I had to wrap the fish in something." He held up the sea bass they were having for dinner. It was wrapped in Jackson's history midterm exam paper and there was a giant, red C-minus in the middle of the paper. "See?" he asked.

"Minus," Miley added with a satisfied smile.

After dinner, Miley sat on the sofa studying algebra. She'd decided to show her dad how hard she was working, so that he'd

change his mind and let her go to the movie with Lilly and Oliver.

Mr Stewart came downstairs, dressed to go out. Jackson trailed behind him, using a different form of persuasion – bad excuses.

"I know, Dad, but what I'm saying is, who really needs history?" Jackson spotted some coins on the kitchen island and slipped them into his pocket. "It's so . . . yesterday," he said. "I'm about the future."

The future? Robby Stewart gave him a look that said, 'How dumb do you think I am?'

"So am I," he answered. "And right now I see you at thirty-five, with no job, living with me, still stealing my loose change off the counter." He held out his hand and Jackson gave him back the money – but not all of it. Mr Stewart whistled and Jackson reached into his other pocket for the rest.

Mr Stewart picked up Jackson's history textbook – the one he hadn't read *before* his midterm – and placed it in Jackson's hands. "This is a book. Go forth and learn."

Miley looked up from her own book. "Remember my 'ha-ha' from before?" she asked, standing up. "I now add one more 'ha', making it a full 'ha-ha' – wait for it – 'ha'!" she sang.

Jackson snapped his book closed and took a step towards Miley, but Mr Stewart came between them. "Anybody seen my PDA?" he asked, looking around for the electronic device that held his diary.

Miley grabbed the Palm Pilot from under her papers on the end table. "Here," she said, handing it to him.

"Thanks." Mr Stewart pressed a couple of buttons and crossed to the kitchen.

Miley followed on his heels. She had to

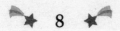

get him to say yes before he went out. "Now, Dad, I know you already said no. But I've been studying so much, I sneezed a while ago and algebra came out."

Mr Stewart didn't budge. "Next time, sneeze a little on your brother. He could use all the help he can get," he said, picking up his mobile phone. "I'm heading out to my meeting. I should be back around eleven. I'll be on my mobile if anybody needs me – so try not to need me." He headed for the door but stopped and turned around with a shake of his head. "I don't know. Do you guys think I'm being too hard on you?"

"Yeah!" Miley and Jackson shouted at the same time.

Mr Stewart nodded. "Good. Because that means I'm doing my job right. Study hard now," he said, walking out of the door.

Chapter Two

Miley couldn't concentrate. She tried studying on the sofa, on the floor and even lying on her stomach on a skateboard. Whether she was right-side up or upside down, she just couldn't get interested in algebra or language arts, not when there was a new Ashton Kutcher movie to be seen. Social studies made her so sleepy that she finally fell over backwards, off the chair and onto the floor.

Jackson was having the same problem. He tried to relieve the boredom by hitting golf balls while he read. The club dangled from his mouth while he held his history book open in front of him. Then he juggled apples with the book on his head. Next he propped it open behind the kitchen tap and practised his jump shot. Oranges doubled as balls and the sink as a basket. Finally he used a hand mirror and coloured markers to draw a face on his belly.

Miley yawned and did a backflip off the couch. "Wow," she said, looking at her watch. "Eight minutes already?"

By now, Jackson had turned his belly button into a mouth and made it talk in a high, squeaky voice. "Yeah. Time to turn in. Good thing I'm not an outie." He used his thumbs to make the belly button laugh.

The doorbell rang. Miley rolled her eyes

and blocked her view of Jackson's stomach with her hand. "Cover him up, we've got company."

"Aw," Jackson said in his belly-button voice. "She don't like me."

Miley opened the front door. Oliver Oken breezed in, followed by Miley's best friend, Lilly Truscott.

Lilly and Oliver were the only two people in the world, except for Jackson and her dad, that Miley trusted with her secret. It was a big one. Miley Stewart led a double life. She was Hannah Montana – a hip, hot, pop-music sensation. Miley loved being Hannah onstage, but offstage she was happy to take off her blonde Hannah wig and pop-star clothes and go back to being Miley Stewart. She wanted people to like her for who she was, not because she was famous. That meant keeping her Hannah self under wraps. Only her best friends and her family knew the real truth.

"So, what's the deal? Did your dad say yes or no?" Oliver asked.

"Yeah, let's get those feet moving," Lilly said. "My mum's in the car grooving to the oldies." She made a disgusted face. "And it's getting uglier by the decade."

Miley broke the bad news. "Lilly, my dad said no."

Lilly wasn't taking no for an answer. Her best bud had to come! "You *think* he said no," she reasoned. "He really said *go*. No. Go," she repeated, demonstrating how much alike the two words sounded. "It's a mistake anybody could make." She grabbed Miley by the hand and tried to drag her to the door. "Come on."

Miley wouldn't budge. "I just can't go."

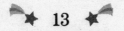 13

"I heard Ashton Kutcher is going to be there," Oliver said, plopping down on the sofa. If that didn't get Miley to change her mind, he knew nothing would.

Miley stamped her foot. "Okay, now you're just being cruel," she said. But she wondered if maybe, just maybe, she should let her friends talk her into going. "That's good," she decided. "It's working. Keep going."

Lilly leaned forwards and whispered in her friend's ear, "Do it. Do it." She spoke in the voice she had used when she played the evil witch in the school production of Hansel and Gretel. Lilly could tell that Miley was about to crumble. "Ashton," Lilly whispered. "Do it."

Miley really wanted to go to the movie, but she had never flat-out ignored her father's rules before. Still, it wasn't fair.

 14

Midterms weren't until next week and everybody else got to go out tonight. Her father was the only spoilsport. "Uh . . . just one more time," she said, hoping that Lilly would push her over the edge.

Lilly wiggled her fingers and spoke in her wicked-witch voice. "Do it."

That did it. Miley would have happily strolled into Lilly's sweet-covered house in the middle of the woods. And besides, she told herself, her father would be out until eleven. He'd never know. She was going. "Okay!" she said.

Oliver gazed at Lilly with admiration. "You, my friend, are wicked good."

Lilly accepted the compliment with a smile. But they still had work to do. "Okay," she said, "all we have to do is sneak you out without Jackson knowing."

Jackson chose that moment to walk

around the kitchen island and show them all his 'new friend'. He held a can of pop up under his stomach and put the straw into his belly button. "Chug! Chug! Chug!" he chanted.

Miley shook her head. "He'll never notice," she said with a laugh. "He's got a friend over." She leaned forwards and whispered her plan in Lilly's ear.

Lilly nodded. "Gotcha."

"I didn't hear." Oliver looked from Miley to Lilly with a blank stare. "Got what?"

Lilly shot him a warning look. Did he want to give them away? "Milk," she said, hoping her tone of voice would warn him from saying any more. She grabbed Oliver by the arm and pulled him to his feet. "I'll tell you in the car," she whispered. Then she spoke loud enough for Jackson to hear. "Okay, well, gotta go."

Oliver tried to help make Jackson think he and Lilly were leaving without Miley. Unfortunately, he was really bad at deception. "Straight home to drink some milk," he said to Jackson, nodding his head. He lowered his voice and turned to Lilly. "How am I doing?" he asked.

"Shut up," Lilly answered, pushing him out of the door.

Miley held her breath for a second, but Jackson was so busy with his new belly-button buddy that he didn't notice Oliver's lame attempt at subterfuge.

"Well, I'm just going to go upstairs and study," Miley said to Jackson, before running up the stairs.

"Well, I'm just going to stay down here and not care," Jackson yelled after her.

Chapter Three

Jackson was watching his sister run up the stairs when his mobile phone rang. He checked the caller ID. It was his friend Cooper. "Oh, yeah, big dawg! Woof, woof, woof! What's up?" Jackson asked.

Cooper was at the cinema, where he had a part-time job as an usher. "Check this out, J-man," he said. "I just found out – wait, hold up." A customer stood in front of him. Cooper checked his ticket. "Theatre three?

I'm guessing it's very close to theatre two," he said sarcastically. "Can't you see I'm on the phone here?"

The customer walked off and Cooper turned his attention back to Jackson. "People. I swear, they're getting more stupid every day," he said.

"Hello! You're costing me minutes here," Jackson said.

Cooper got to the point. "You've got to get down here," he said. "I'm telling you this on the D.L.," he said, using the code for 'down low'. In other words, it was top secret. Then Cooper noticed an elderly woman with a walking frame glance at him. Was she listening? "Keep the walking frame moving, lady," he said, waving his arm. "If you were supposed to hear, I'd be on speakerphone." As soon as she was out of earshot, he lowered his voice and spoke into the phone again.

"There's a very hot rumour that Mr Ashton Kutcher is dropping by here tonight."

Jackson didn't understand. Miley and Lilly were the big Ashton fans, not him. "And I should care about this because?" he asked.

"Because, this place is going to be crawling with fine ladies wanting to get next to Ashton. And when they can't find him . . ."

Now Jackson got it.

"They'll settle for us!" Jackson and Cooper shouted at the same time, pumping their fists in the air. "Oh, yeah!" they said together.

"So you feel me on this?" Cooper asked.

"I don't know, Coop," he said, feeling disappointed. "If I split, Miley's going to tell Dad." He thought about it for a minute. "Of course, she is in her room for the rest of the night."

Upstairs, Miley had dropped a rope ladder from her bedroom window to the porch below. It dangled outside the window right behind Jackson.

But Jackson had his back turned to the window. "And she's such a goody-goody," Jackson continued. "Little Miss Perfect. Always sucking up to Dad," he complained. "Just once in her life you'd think she'd go out on a limb or something. But will she? No. Because she's gutless."

Miley heard her brother's every word. She was not Little Miss Perfect! She shook her fist at Jackson's back and stuck her tongue out at him before running off to join Lilly and Oliver. She'd show him 'gutless'.

Jackson was oblivious to Miley's secret getaway. "You know what?" he said to Cooper. "She'll never know I'm gone. I just talked me into it." He dashed upstairs to change into something Ashton Kutcher fans would go for.

Jackson and Cooper walked through the cinema. The place was crawling with pretty girls.

"Cooper, you are a genius," Jackson told his friend. "It's like cheerleader tryouts."

"Right." Cooper nodded. "Except we don't have to wear those itchy man sweaters and do the splits. You know I still can't ride a bike?"

Jackson shook his head. "Ah, the things we do for love."

The friends turned to each other with huge smiles. Their craziest adventures all had something to do with girls. "Oh, yeah!" they said together, then slid their right palms against each other's, knocked their fists, snapped their fingers and tapped their knees – it was their secret handshake.

"Now," Cooper said, "how to proceed is the question."

Jackson already had a plan. "Watch and learn," he said and swaggered over to a group of girls with his mobile phone in his hand. "Hey, Ashton!" he said into the phone. "Mr Kutcher. My man!"

The girls didn't notice. Jackson moved closer and talked louder. "The Kutchinator!" he yelled. "Kutchy, Kutchy you."

The girls stopped munching on their popcorn and listened. Soon they were talking to each other in excited whispers. More girls joined them.

"What's that, my close personal friend?" Jackson asked. He checked out the girls. Every single one of them was flashing him an eager smile. This was the best plan he had ever come up with! "Come to your party tonight?" he yelled into the phone.

The girls leaned forward. Every single one of them wanted to be Jackson's date to that party.

"Sure," Jackson said, enjoying the attention. "I'll find myself a little hottie, and we'll party like it's—"

Unfortunately, Jackson hadn't remembered to turn off his phone. It rang just as the girls were about to start throwing themselves at him. Now they all knew Jackson was a total poser.

"Hello?" Jackson said, his voice cracking with embarrassment. "Hey, Barry. Can I give you a call back?"

The girls groaned and turned away.

"Ladies?" Jackson called after them. But they had already moved on.

Cooper laughed in the background.

"Very smooth," he teased, throwing his arm around Jackson's shoulder. "I was watching and learning and what I learned is I should *not* have watched."

Jackson laughed, too. "All right, have a little patience, my man," he said. "It's just a minor setback." He spotted a couple of girls across the lobby with their backs to him. "Prepare to be impressed."

Jackson made sure his phone was turned off this time. He strolled across the lobby, followed by Cooper. "So," he said, as soon as he was within the girls' hearing range. "Mr Kutcher. The Kutch King. Volcanic Ash!"

The girls turned around. It was Miley and Lilly! Jackson and Miley both screamed in outrage when they spotted each other.

Cooper shook his head. "At this rate, I've

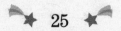

got a better chance with that lady with the walking frame. I bet she hasn't passed theatre five yet," he joked, before leaving to take care of some of his usher duties.

"What are *you* doing here?" Jackson yelled.

"Me?" Miley pointed at her brother. "What about you?"

"I'm telling Dad!" they said, their words overlapping.

They glared at each other for a second.

"No, you're not," they said, again at the same time.

Jackson nodded. "Because we're not here right now," he said.

"Right," Miley agreed. She wouldn't tell on Jackson if her brother didn't tell on her. So they *weren't* there.

But just then, she looked across the lobby, and what she saw made her gasp in shock. "But Dad is!"

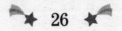

Chapter Four

Miley grabbed Jackson's arm and pulled him behind a giant cardboard cutout of a smiling family – an advertisement for a new movie. A second later, she pulled Lilly in, too. The three of them huddled behind the poster.

Jackson shook his head sadly and talked to himself. "What can I say, Dad? She sneaked out. I followed her here. I'm just as disappointed as you are."

"What are you doing?" Miley snapped.

"What does it look like I'm doing?" Jackson asked. "I'm getting ready to sell you out."

"Listen, buster." Miley waved her finger in her brother's face. "If I go down, I'm taking you with me." She poked her head out from behind the cardboard cutout. Her father was munching on popcorn in front of theatre two. Miley ducked down again. "What is he doing here?" she asked, exasperated. "He said he had a meeting."

"All right, just calm down," Lilly said, matter-of-factly. "All we have to do is wait until he goes in. He'll never know you were here." But Lilly had forgotten all about Oliver and he was about to give them away.

Oliver wandered through the lobby with his extra-large popcorn, looking for his friends. "Lilly?" he called. "Miley?"

Lilly yanked Oliver behind the cutout. His popcorn went flying.

"Aw, man!" Oliver said.

"Miley's dad is here," Lilly explained.

"Great," Oliver said. He liked Mr Stewart. Oliver started to get up to say hello, but Miley pulled him back behind the cutout.

"He doesn't know we're here," Miley reminded him. "We'd like to keep it that way." But now it was Miley's turn to almost give them away. She accidentally nudged the poster with her foot and it fell over.

There they were, crouched on the floor in plain sight of Mr Stewart! He turned in their direction and started reading movie posters just as they got the cutout standing upright again.

Miley hated hiding like this and she really didn't want to get into trouble. "We have got to get out of here," she whispered.

The four of them picked up the cutout and started moving away from Mr Stewart and towards the exit, inch by inch.

Suddenly, Miley realized that she had left her handbag behind. She peeked out from between the cardboard family's heads. Her bag was right next to Robby Stewart's foot! "Wait!" she whispered. "My bag."

They inched back in the direction of Mr Stewart. Miley held her breath and reached under the poster. She almost grabbed her father's leg. But then she got her hands on the bag and they started to back up again.

They were creeping away when Jackson's mobile phone rang. He checked the caller ID. "It's Dad. He must be calling to check in."

The kids peeked around the cardboard heads. Suddenly the family of six in the ad became a family of ten. Robby checked his watch and read movie posters while he waited for Jackson to answer his phone.

"Don't answer it," Miley urged. "Keep moving."

"I have to answer it. He thinks we're at home." Jackson punched the talk button and answered in a loud, cheerful voice. "Hey, Dad. We're at home."

Miley leaned over his shoulder and joined in. "Studying, at home."

"Where we are," Jackson added. "Home . . ."

"Sweet home!" Miley sang into the phone.

"Home," they both said together.

"I just called to check in on you guys and let you know that whatever it is that you're doin' that you don't want me to know you're doin' – stop doin' it," Mr Stewart drawled in his Tennessee accent.

He walked up and down in front of the posters while he talked. The kids had to keep turning the poster to stay hidden.

"Study hard now," Mr Stewart said. "Bye." He snapped his phone closed and walked back to theatre two.

Miley grimaced. She felt horribly guilty. Her father believed that she and Jackson were at home, not studying maybe, but at home. "I *hate* lying to him," she said.

As far as Lilly was concerned, it was way too late to be worried about lying. Right now, they needed to concentrate on getting out of there before Miley got into too much trouble. Miley could feel guilty tomorrow, when she wasn't in danger of getting caught and of being grounded. "You're on your hands and knees in a movie theatre," she said. "The honesty ship has sailed."

Oliver turned to Lilly. "I just can't figure out one thing — why are *we* hiding?"

"Oliver, you naive, simple boy," Lilly answered, then realized he was right, "with a great idea." She didn't have to miss Ashton Kutcher's sneak preview. Miley did. "Best of luck," she said to Miley with a smile, before grabbing Oliver's arm and racing to the preview.

Miley threw up her hands in frustration. She had sneaked out of the house and lied to her father and now her best friends had left her while she crouched on the floor of the cinema. "Perfect," she said to Jackson. "Could this night get any worse?"

Jackson was checking out his father's movements from behind the poster. He watched an attractive woman walk up to Mr Stewart. They were talking and smiling. Could things get worse? "Depends on how you feel about *that*," Jackson answered.

Miley's head popped up in time to see the woman take a handful of Mr Stewart's popcorn and laugh at one of his jokes. Her eyes widened in shock. "I don't believe it."

"I know," Jackson agreed with a shake of his head. "The old man can get a date and I can't."

Miley's heart plunged into her stomach. She watched, stunned, as the woman took Robby Stewart's arm. They strolled together into the cinema, looking exactly like a couple on a date.

Miley forgot about the Ashton Kutcher movie. All she could think about was the fact that her father was on a date. How could he, she wondered. How could her father go on a date and not tell her?

Chapter Five

Miley paced back and forth in the kitchen while Jackson munched on a giant sandwich. "Why would Dad do this?" she asked. "Why did he go on a date and not tell us?"

"I don't know," Jackson answered, his mouth full of ham and cheese.

Miley stopped pacing and watched her brother take another giant bite – he hadn't even swallowed the first one yet! "Please stop stuffing your face!" she pleaded. Did Jackson know how serious this was?

"I'm eating away the pain," Jackson said between chews.

Miley rolled her eyes and then got serious. "Doesn't this bother you?" she asked.

"Miley," Jackson said softly, "it's been three years. He's probably lonely."

Three years or not, Miley was not ready for her father to date. "Then we'll get him a puppy!" she said, hearing a car door close outside. "I hear him."

Miley headed for the front door.

Jackson followed her. "Look, just remember that whatever happens, he can't know we were there," Jackson reminded his sister. "So play it cool."

"I will, I will," Miley said over her shoulder. "He won't suspect a thing."

Miley shook off her nervous tension, the way she did when she was about to go onstage as Hannah Montana.

Mr Stewart came in whistling.

"Where have you been?" Miley yelled. "We agreed home by eleven. And it's—"

Mr Stewart checked his watch. "Eleven oh three."

"Exactly!" Miley said. "Three minutes of pure agony."

Jackson saw that Miley was so far from playing it cool that she was practically boiling. He put his arm around her to get her to stop talking before she got them both grounded. "Yes, but the important thing is that while you were out, we weren't," Jackson said firmly.

Miley got the message. Or did she? "Right," she said. "And you were at a meeting. How did that go?"

"Fine," her father answered.

"Fine? One syllable? That's all I get?"

Mr Stewart's forehead wrinkled in confusion. Since when did Miley want to know about his meetings? "Okay. It was really fine," he teased. "That's three syllables. Keep the change."

But Miley wasn't satisfied with 'really fine'. She put her hand over her heart and focused on her father's brown eyes. "Dad, you're always talking about how we don't share enough. Well, you're right. And we should." She got down to business. "Starting now. You go first."

Her father relented. "Okay. It was a very–" he fumbled for a word that wouldn't give away his secret, "–*productive* meeting, and who knows, in time it could amount to a little something."

Jackson eyed Miley. Even he didn't like

the sound of that. "Like what?" he asked.

"You know, talking about things too early might jinx it," Mr Stewart said. "Don't worry, if it keeps going the way it's going, I'll tell you all about it." He kissed Miley on the forehead and squeezed Jackson's shoulder. "Love you, guys. Good night."

"Love you, too," Miley said sadly, watching her father climb the stairs. As soon as he was out of earshot, she turned to Jackson. "Well, great, this is terrible," she snapped. "He's happy."

The next morning, Miley stopped pacing long enough to sit across the breakfast table from Lilly. Her imagination ran wild. "I just wish I knew something about this woman. *Anything*," Miley said. She ticked off a list of questions. "What does she do for a living? Does she have any kids? Any dogs? A soundproof basement where no one can hear our screams? I don't even know her name."

Jackson walked over with his father's Palm Pilot. "Margo Diamond," he said.

"What?" Miley asked.

"'Movie, Saturday night'," Jackson read. "Margo Diamond." Jackson thought that name sounded familiar. Suddenly he realized where he had heard it before. "Hey, she's that estate agent. You know, the one on the bus bench in front of the library."

Lilly gasped. "Your dad's dating a homeless estate agent? Wow, that's weird. She sells houses, but she doesn't have one."

"I meant the ad on the bench, Ms Einstein," Jackson scoffed.

Lilly ignored Jackson's insult. She had already come up with a plan to get the answers to all of Miley's questions. "This is perfect," she said. "Now you can go and meet her. Jackson can drive you."

Miley perked up. Lilly was right. She could go and check out this Margo Diamond person and make sure she was good enough for her dad.

"Let me paint you a picture." Jackson grabbed an apple and an orange from the fruit bowl on the table. He pretended the orange was talking. "Hi, I'm Miley Stewart," he said in a high, squeaky voice. "And I'm her brother, Jackson," he said, deepening his voice and waving the apple. "We sneaked out to a movie last night where we saw you on a date with our father. Why are we telling you this? Out of an insane desire to get caught and grounded for the rest of our natural lives!"

Miley rolled her eyes and stalled for time

while she tried to come up with a reason to prove that Jackson was wrong. "Why do you always get to be the apple?" she asked.

"Wait a minute, belly-button boy makes sense," Lilly said.

"Okay, maybe you are right. Maybe we can't go down there and talk to her." Miley's face lit up again when she thought of a new plan. "But I know someone who can," she said with a grin.

Chapter Six

Miley walked into the estate agent's office wearing her blonde Hannah Montana wig and her glittery Hannah clothes. Jackson followed. He was dressed in a dark suit and dark sunglasses. It was the closest thing he had to a chauffeur's uniform.

"This is the most stupid thing I've ever done for you," Jackson said, slipping his shades into his pocket.

Miley rolled her eyes and turned to him.

"This is the *only* thing you've ever done for me." She spotted her dad's date at a desk at the back of the room. "And don't pretend you're not the least bit interested in our future possible stepmum," she said in a whisper.

"Of course I am," Jackson said. "You're not the only one who cares about Dad. I want him to be happy, too."

"All right," Miley said. "Let's do this." She took a deep breath, squared her shoulders and headed for Ms Diamond's desk.

"Just remember, you're my chauffeur," she whispered to Jackson before greeting her new possible stepmum. "Um, hi," she said, stumbling over her words. She felt more like regular Miley than confident pop star Hannah at that moment. "I'm Hannah Montana and I'm looking for a house."

Ms Diamond laughed and jotted a note on the pad on her desk. "That's the stupidest thing I've ever heard."

Jackson stepped forwards to defend his sister. "Lady, you're not going to sell many houses with that attitude."

Miley nodded in agreement. How could her father date this woman? she wondered. She was rude and insulting!

Ms Diamond turned around and pointed to her headset to indicate that she was on the phone. "We'll talk later," she said, walking around her desk to greet Miley. Now Ms Diamond was the one stumbling over her words. "Sorry. Telephone. Hi." She reached out to shake Miley's hand with an embarrassed laugh. "What a thrill to meet you. My niece is a big fan of yours."

"Really?" Jackson asked, jumping in

front of his sister. "How old is she? What does she look like? And do you happen to have a picture of her?"

"Not why we're here," Miley warned Jackson through clenched teeth. She turned to Ms Diamond with a beaming Hannah Montana smile and got down to business. "But if we are going to be in business together, I need to know a little bit about you first. For example, who's this?"

Miley picked up a picture from Ms Diamond's desk. Her tone totally changed when she saw that it was a picture of a man. "Your husband? Does he know you're dating?"

Ms Diamond looked at Miley in amazement. "Wait a minute. That's my brother."

"A likely story." Miley nudged Jackson.

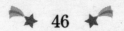

"Who keeps a picture of their brother on their desk?" she asked.

"He gave me a kidney," Ms Diamond said firmly.

Miley put her hand over her heart and turned back to Ms Diamond. "So you're scarred," she said.

"You know, this is getting kind of personal. Can we stick to houses?" Ms Diamond moved around behind her desk and tried to sit.

"Certainly," Miley agreed. "What's yours like?"

She and Jackson followed Ms Diamond around her desk and started rummaging through her papers and her drawers, looking for clues to her personal life. "Any kids running around?" Miley asked.

"Daughters who like pillow fights?" Jackson asked hopefully.

Ms Diamond's confusion gave way to anger. She threw her arms out and leaned over her desk to stop them from getting their hands on any of her papers. "Maybe I'm not the right person to sell you a house," she said.

Miley and Jackson reluctantly stepped back.

"Let me put you in touch with Habib, Prince of the West Side." Ms Diamond flipped through her Rolodex, looking for his phone number. There was no way she would let this crazy pop star invade her personal life just to sell a house. "You're going to love him."

"Wait, I'm not finished yet," Miley said. She hadn't learned nearly enough about this woman. What if she wasn't right for Miley's father? Even worse, what if she was?

Jackson looked up. His eyes almost popped out of his head. He tapped Miley on the shoulder and pointed. Their father had just walked through the front door, carrying a bouquet of flowers!

"On second thoughts, yes I am."

Miley dropped to the floor and dragged Jackson with her. She spotted a cupboard behind Ms Diamond's desk and crawled towards it. "Ms Diamond, excuse me and my chauffeur. We have to confer, in private," she said, quickly. "And I must insist that you tell no one I'm here." She closed the cupboard door behind them.

"Absolutely," Ms Diamond said, loudly. She dialled Habib and said more quietly to herself, "I'm trying to forget it myself."

In the cupboard, Jackson practised his sad head-shaking and his explanation. "I don't know what to say, Dad. It was her idea. I tried to stop her. I'm just as disappointed as you are."

"I'm amazed you can stand without a spine," Miley hissed. She had her ear pressed up against the cupboard door, but she couldn't hear!

In the office, Robby Stewart approached Ms Diamond's desk with the flowers. "Hi," he said shyly. "I brought you these."

"Oh, please," Ms Diamond laughed. "I think we can spend a little more money than that!"

Mr Stewart stepped back. "I don't think that's fair," he drawled. "There was the movie last night, popcorn. You wanted the big drink."

"No, no, no," Ms Diamond whispered, pointing to her headset. "I'm on the phone." She took the flowers and placed them on her desk. "These are lovely." Her voice got louder as she talked into the headset again. "Let me call you back."

Miley strained to hear, but she was distracted by a terrible pain in her left foot. "Jackson, you're on my foot!" Miley said.

"I can't move. I've got a FOR SALE sign—" he grimaced, struggling to come up with a good explanation of where it was, "—in my back garden," he said finally.

Miley was able to slide the door open far enough to poke her head out. She was just in time to hear her father's conversation with Ms Diamond.

"I had a nice time last night," said Mr Stewart with a bashful smile.

Margo smiled back. "So did I."

"Man, he really likes her," Miley said, leaning back and closing the cupboard door.

"You know, Mile, she does seem pretty nice," Jackson said.

But Miley wasn't ready to think about her father dating. And she really wasn't ready to like anyone he dated, nice or not. "I don't care how nice she is," Miley snapped. "She's never getting any of my kidneys!"

Back in the office, Miley's father asked Ms Diamond out for coffee.

"I'd love to go out for coffee," she said. "Let me just get someone to cover for me." She started to move away but stopped to let Mr Stewart in on her secret. "You're not going to believe this, but I have got Hannah Montana hiding in my cupboard."

"Huh?" Mr Stewart asked, shocked.

"Yeah, she's what we call half a bath short of a condo," Ms Diamond said, pointing to her head in the universal signal for crazy. She shook her head. "I blame the parents."

Robby nodded grimly. "Yeah, me too."

Chapter Seven

Mr Stewart waited until Ms Diamond had gone to get her coat and was out of hearing range before he walked up to the cupboard. "All right, come on out. Now," he demanded.

Jackson slid the door open and tried to come up with a good explanation. "Aw, Dad, what a relief! You'd never believe how lost I was."

Mr Stewart stared angrily. He wasn't buying that excuse.

"Would it help if I said I was happy for you?" Jackson asked hopefully.

Miley didn't see any reason to try to come up with an excuse or pretend to be happy. She was too hurt and too angry. It was bad enough that her father had gone out on a date, but the fact that he had kept it a secret from her was even worse. She slid open the cupboard's other door and stormed past Mr Stewart. "How could you?" she asked.

Mr Stewart tried to stop her. "Whoa, now hold up, little girl."

Miley whirled around with her hands on her hips.

"How'd you find out?" Mr Stewart asked.

"Well, you didn't tell me," Miley said. She turned her back on him and headed for the door.

Mr Stewart followed. "I can explain."

Miley's anger whooshed out of her. All that was left was a terrible sadness. She fought back tears. "Okay, explain this: why are you dating someone without telling me? Explain how you could think there's someone out there who could ever replace my mum?"

As far as Miley was concerned, there was no explanation for that. She didn't wait to hear what her father had to say. She left.

Mr Stewart turned to Jackson.

"That was awkward," Jackson said. He had planned to follow Miley out of the office, but the expression on his father's face stopped him. Jackson decided it was better to hide. He stepped back into the cupboard and closed the door.

That night, Miley sat on the porch strumming her guitar and thinking about her mother. She looked at the stars and smiled sadly. Was her mother looking down at her? Miley started to sing the song she had written after her mother passed away. After a few lines, she noticed that her father had joined her.

"That's a beautiful song, honey," he said.

Miley turned away. She couldn't look at him. She was too upset.

"I like coming out here at night," Mr Stewart said. "It's a good place to try to figure things out."

Miley stared straight ahead, refusing to speak to him.

"Maybe we could figure things out together," he said.

"Why didn't you tell me?" Miley demanded.

"I guess I was hoping to tell you at just the right time and in just the right way, so you'd understand . . . and not end up out here on the porch, all alone," her father said. His voice softened. "I guess there was no right time, was there?"

Miley stood and paced across the porch. She leaned against the railing, gazing at the stars and the ocean waves. "I just can't picture you with anybody else but Mum," she said, blinking back tears.

"Neither can I. What she and I had was special. I can't replace that," her father answered.

"Then why are you dating?" Miley asked. It didn't make any sense to her.

"Because life goes on," Mr Stewart answered. "I've got to figure out some way to go on with it. Don't you think your mum would've wanted that for us?"

Miley thought that over. More than anything else, she knew her mother would want them all to live the happiest lives they could. But Miley still didn't feel ready to see her father date anyone else. "Yeah, I guess she would have. She was pretty wise that way. I really miss her, Daddy."

"I miss her too, kiddo," Mr Stewart said gently.

Miley and her father hugged tightly. They held each other for a moment and then Mr Stewart spotted the rope ladder on the deck. It looked suspiciously like Miley's emergency fire ladder.

"What's this rope ladder doing here?" he asked.

"Uh, Dad," Miley smiled, hugging him harder and trying to kick the rope away. "Let's not ruin this beautiful moment."

Her father thought about it for a second. "You're right. I'll ruin it tomorrow."

Miley hugged him again. She'd always miss her mother, but she knew her father loved her and was there for her, now and forever.

PART TWO

Chapter One

Miley and Lilly were hanging out at Rico's Surf Shop, a snack shack near the beach. Jackson was behind the counter. He was supposed to be working, but really he was hanging out, too. Cooper had just stopped by for some nachos.

Miley gazed at something in the distance with a small smile on her face. She absentmindedly worked her way through Cooper's nachos.

Cooper stared in disbelief. "Girl, you sure like nachos," he said. "Problem is, they're not your nachos."

Miley kept eating, totally oblivious to Cooper's growing frustration.

"Yo!" Cooper yelled. He tapped Miley on the shoulder, trying to get her attention.

It didn't work. Miley chomped away on crisp after crisp. She couldn't take her eyes off the totally amazing sight across the beach. She had an expression of pure bliss on her face.

"She can't hear you," Jackson explained. He pointed to a guy in a wetsuit showering the sand off at the outdoor beach shower. "She's enjoying the all-you-can-eat *lurrrvvvv*e buffet."

Lilly agreed. She'd seen Miley go into trances like this before and there was usually a cute guy involved. "It's true," she

Part One

"The new Ashton Kutcher movie is previewing tonight!
How many 'pretty's do I need to put before 'please' for you
to let me go?" Miley asked.

"You know you've got to study," said Mr Stewart.
Midterms were coming up, and he wanted to make sure
Miley and her brother, Jackson, did well.

"You *think* he said no," Lilly reasoned when Miley told her
that she wasn't allowed to go to the movie preview. "He really said *go*. It's a mistake anybody could make."

When Jackson got invited to the same movie preview, he
wasn't sure if he should sneak out. He didn't know that Miley
was already on her way!

The two decided to keep each other's secret, until they got a big surprise. Their dad was at the movie, too!

"Hey, Dad, we're at home," said Jackson.
"Studying – at home," Miley chimed in.

"I *hate* lying to him," Miley said.
"You're on your hands and knees in a movie
theatre," Lilly said. "The honesty ship has sailed!"

It turned out that Miley's dad had been at the cinema on a
date. But who could she be? Jackson walked over with his
father's Palm Pilot. "Margo Diamond," he said.

Part Two

When Hannah refused to ask Josh out, Lilly gave
her a pep talk. "You're Hannah
'Teen Pop Sensation' Montana!"

"Hello, Josh Woods!" Miley yelled in her strong
Hannah voice. "You ready to rock tonight?!"

"What?" Josh was totally confused. Why was Miley Stewart yelling at him as if he were a crowd of thousands?

"Sorry, Josh," Mr Stewart told Josh when he called Miley that night. "She's in the bathroom."

"Do you realize how much easier life was when she believed boys had fleas?" Mr Stewart asked.

"I can't believe it. I'm going out with a ninth grader!" Miley exclaimed.

"I cannot believe I just blew it,"
Miley said to her best friend, Lilly.

Mr Stewart sat down next to them.
"Well, as far as I'm concerned, that's his loss."

said. "When she's like this, she doesn't know what she's doing. I'll show you." Lilly rolled a serviette into a ball and dropped it on top of the nachos.

Miley popped the serviette into her mouth as if it were a crisp and kept chewing. She didn't even notice that her latest treat was made of paper.

"Miley!" Lilly yelled, pulling the serviette out of her best friend's mouth.

That finally got Miley's attention. "What?" she asked, slightly annoyed. Why was Lilly talking to her when Josh Woods was standing just a short distance away? Didn't Lilly notice how cute he was?

Lilly didn't get it. Why didn't Miley take matters into her own hands instead of waiting around for Josh to notice her? "Just go ask Josh out," Lilly said.

Miley shook her head. "I'm from

Tennessee," Miley said. "We don't do that."

"Well, you're in California now and we *do* do that."

Jackson and Cooper cracked up.

"What?" Lilly asked.

"You said 'do do'," Jackson said, laughing.

The girls looked at each other and rolled their eyes.

"Grow up!" Miley said, throwing her hands up into the air.

"You're the one who can't ask a guy out," Jackson teased.

Jackson really didn't get it, Miley thought. "He's not just a guy. He's a ninth grader," Miley explained. "I can't just put eighth-grade moves on him."

"Good point," Lilly said. "And besides, he probably doesn't even know you're alive. You're like some dried-up insect on the windscreen of his life."

Jackson and Cooper cracked up again. Miley wondered if her friend was trying to help her or hurt her.

Lilly kept going with her insect-on-the-windscreen comparison. "Not even the centre. You're way off to the side where the wipers don't reach." Lilly waved her arms back and forth and imitated the sound of windscreen wipers. "Squeak, squeak, squeak, splat. Squeak, squeak, squeak, splat." The splat was Miley.

"Lilly," Miley said.

"What?"

"This is officially the worst pep talk ever," Miley told her.

"You want a pep talk?" Lilly asked. She pulled Miley away from the snack counter so Cooper wouldn't hear her. "You're

Hannah 'Teen Pop Sensation' Montana," Lilly reminded her. "You're going to go out in front of thousands of people on Saturday night. Just pretend he's one of them."

Miley realized her friend was right. She was super-confident in her role as Hannah. Whenever she put on her blonde Hannah wig and her glittery Hannah clothes, she was transformed from a regular eighth grader into a pop star. She had no problem singing to thousands of people on the concert stage. In fact, she loved it. So why couldn't she ask out a guy like Josh?

"You're right," Miley agreed. "That's all he is. One guy. I can do this," she told Lilly. "I'll just channel Hannah." She headed in Josh's direction and found herself in front of him just as he finished towelling off. Their eyes met. Miley froze under Josh's questioning gaze.

Channel Hannah, she chanted to herself, channel Hannah. Miley flashed him her biggest, whitest Hannah smile. But instead of talking to just one guy, she sounded as if she were shouting to a crowded arena. "Hello, Josh Woods!" she yelled in her strong Hannah voice. "You ready to rock tonight?!"

"What?" Josh was totally confused. Why was Miley Stewart yelling at him as if he were a crowd of thousands?

Miley was mortified. That was way over the top. But she was in full Hannah mode and couldn't seem to stop. "Thank you!" Miley shouted. "Good night, everybody!"

She ran to back to Lilly and pulled her off the beach – away from the scene of her humiliation.

Chapter Two

Miley ranted about the scene with Josh all through dinner, acting out the worst parts. "Then I ate a serviette and then Jackson was all 'you said do do' and then Lilly was all 'insect on the windshield' and then I was all, 'good night, everybody!' And that's why we have to move." She couldn't get her embarrassment off her mind. Josh must think that she was the biggest idiot in the world.

But Robby Stewart wasn't buying her logic. They couldn't just move every time Miley was embarrassed about something. "Sorry, darling," he said with a shake of his head. The phone rang, and he got up to answer it while Jackson chuckled, remembering Miley's meltdown on the beach. It was too funny.

"What?" Miley demanded.

"Nothing," Jackson said with a smile.

"Hello . . . hold on," Mr Stewart said into the phone. "Mile, it's for you."

Miley waved him off. What if it was someone who had heard about the disaster at the beach? Whoever it was could gloat another time. "I can't talk to anyone right now. Could you just make something up?"

"Sorry, Josh," Mr Stewart said. "She's in the bathroom."

Miley's eyes almost popped out of her

head. Josh? Josh Woods? And her father had said she was in the bathroom!

"It could be a while," her father continued.

"No!" Miley screamed, jumping to her feet.

"Hold on, sounds like she's coming," Mr Stewart said.

Jackson cracked up.

"Give me that phone," Miley said through clenched teeth. Her angry tone turned super-sweet when she grabbed the receiver. "Hi. This is Miley."

Mr Stewart sat down with a chuckle while Miley moved out of earshot.

"'It could be a while,'" Jackson repeated with a laugh. "You, sir, do not know how good you are."

"Next time, I'm letting the machine pick up," his father answered. Mr Stewart didn't necessarily love the idea of boys calling his daughter. "Do you realize how much easier life was when she believed boys had fleas?"

"Yes!" Miley sang, hanging up the phone. She bounced over to the table, her embarrassment totally forgotten. "I can't believe it. I'm going out with a ninth grader! Woo-hoo!" She pumped her fist in the air.

"Don't believe it, because I'm not letting you! Woo-hoo!" her father answered, pumping his own fist in the air.

"But, Daddy," Miley whined.

"But nothing. He's a year older. In teenage boy years that adds up to . . ." he pretended to do maths in the air, ". . . let's see, carry the one, equals . . . ain't going to happen."

"This is so unfair," Miley said, pushing

her bottom lip out into a pout and gazing at her father with her big brown eyes. It had worked when she was five and wanted a biscuit. Why not try it now, she thought.

"Sad face," Mr Stewart said, pointing at her and making one himself.

Miley nodded and pushed her bottom lip out a little farther.

Her father's expression went from sad to one that said, "I mean business." He pointed at his own face. "Not-buying-it face," he said.

Miley crossed her arms over her chest and marched upstairs.

Jackson tried to help his sister. "C'mon, Dad. It wasn't that long ago that I was a ninth grader. And if he's anything like I was . . ." Jackson's eyes got wide, remembering his ninth-grade self. "You need to meet that boy!"

By the next day, Mr Stewart had surrendered. Miley could go out with Josh – if Mr Stewart met him first and approved. He strummed an acoustic guitar while Miley bounced around, waiting for Josh to arrive.

She rushed in from the porch. "He's coming up the path," she said excitedly. "He is so cute! But we've got to be calm. Just be calm," she told her father.

Mr Stewart didn't share his daughter's excitement. "Honey, if I was any calmer, I'd be dead."

That reminded Miley. Her father was always making lame jokes, like that one. She had to get him not to do that in front of Josh. It would be too embarrassing. "Dad, big favour, don't try to be funny with Josh. Because you aren't funny."

"I don't know. I crack myself up all the time." Just to prove his point, her father told a joke. "What do you call a pig that knows karate?" he asked. "Pork chop! Ha!" he said, slicing the air with a karate chop.

Miley rolled her eyes while her father laughed at his own joke. He was definitely going to embarrass her in front of Josh. "Daddy, please, I'm begging you," she pleaded. "Don't talk." She climbed over the back of the sofa and struck a pose, resting her head casually on one hand, with the other hand on her hip. "I'm just going to sit here and look casual, like I live here all the time."

"Good thinking," Mr Stewart said, amused.

"Hey, Miley," Josh smiled at her from the open front door. His eyes were focused on Miley. He didn't see Mr Stewart. "Whoa, you look hot," Josh said.

Miley fluffed her hair and gave Josh a beaming smile.

Robby Stewart stood up. "Hi, I'm the hot chick's father. How do I look?" he asked, suddenly not amused.

Uh-oh! Josh cleared his throat. He looked at Miley for clues, but she was just as horrified by her father's question as he was. "Very handsome, sir," he said finally.

"Nice try," Mr Stewart said, softening slightly. "Now take your foot out of your mouth, come in here and let's start again." He offered Josh his hand.

Josh rushed in to shake hands, stumbling over his words. "Yes, sir. Thank you, sir. I'm Josh Woods, sir."

Miley had to put a stop to this or her first

date with Josh would be over before it started. "Well, you've met, you've bonded, 'nuff said." She took Josh's arm. "Bye-bye!" she sang, trying to hurry Josh back to the beach.

Mr Stewart wasn't letting go of Josh's hand. "Whoa, whoa, whoa, not so fast," he said.

But Miley was determined to get Josh out of there. Two things could happen – her father could totally embarrass her by telling bad jokes or totally embarrass her by deciding he didn't like Josh and making her stay at home. She had to put a stop to this ASAP. "Why 'not so fast'?" she asked. "Fast is good. Fast food, fast lane, fast forward – bye-bye," Miley said again, leading Josh to the door.

"Whoa," Josh said, catching sight of Mr Stewart's guitars. "Cool guitars."

"Oh, you like guitars, do you?" Mr Stewart asked.

"Oh, yeah. These are pretty good ones," Josh said, picking up the acoustic guitar. "Not as good as a Diefenbacher, but you know that."

Was this kid trying to tell Robby Stewart about guitars? "No, I don't know that," Mr Stewart said, clearly insulted.

There goes the other foot, Miley said to herself. No one knew more about guitars than her father, especially not a ninth grader. This wasn't going to be pretty.

Josh could tell he had said something totally wrong. "Look, sir," he said, picking up the acoustic guitar. "I'm not saying this wasn't a good guitar in its day."

Mr Stewart didn't let him finish. "In its day? Sounds like you've been a musician for a long time. Like, thirty years," he said sarcastically. "Oh, wait, that's me."

Miley had to stop this before it turned into a complete and total disaster and they really would have to move. Miley stepped between them. "Isn't that interesting? You have your opinion and he has his," she said, turning from her father to Josh and back again. "You've got to love a guy who isn't afraid to say how he feels."

"I'm a little afraid to say anything right now," Josh said.

"No, you're not," Miley said, trying to turn Josh's foot-in-mouth episode into a positive thing. "If everybody says that they like hamburgers, he's not afraid to say that he likes hot dogs, right?" she asked, nodding at Josh.

"Okay," Josh said, confused.

"And some people like skiing and he's

not afraid to say that he likes snowboarding."

Josh was getting it now. "Yeah," he said, trying to think of another example. He picked up a teen magazine that was lying on the table. Hannah Montana's smiling face was on the front cover. "Some people like Hannah Montana, and I'm not afraid to say she stinks."

"Abso–" Miley started to agree and then his words sank in. "What?" she asked, totally stunned. How could Josh hate Hannah? *She* was Hannah!

"Son of a gun," Mr Stewart said, putting his arm around Miley. "The boy's got three feet."

Chapter Three

Jackson stood behind the counter at Rico's Surf Shop. Business was slow and none of his friends had stopped by. He tried on a pair of dark sunglasses from the display on the counter. "Hello, I am the Jackson-ator," he said, imitating Arnold Schwarzenegger from the *Terminator* movies.

He studied himself in the mirror. These were not the shades for him. He wasn't the

Terminator type. "You will *not* be back," he said, taking them off. He tried a small, blue-tinted pair next. "Whoa, rock 'n' roll!" he said, imitating the confused rock star Ozzy Osbourne. "Sharon!"

He looked up to see a beautiful girl with long dark hair laughing at him. "Are you always this funny?" she asked with a big smile.

Jackson's eyes widened. He did a double take to make sure she was talking to him. This girl was not only beautiful, she thought he was funny! "That depends," he said. "Do you like funny?

She flipped her hair over her shoulder. There was a flower tucked behind her ear. "I love funny," she flirted.

"Well, then I am hysterical. Did you hear the one about the pig who knows karate?" he asked.

"Pork chop!" said the girl, laughing.

"Ha!" They karate-chopped the air at the same time.

Jackson was amazed – beauty and a sense of humour in one package. "Can you spell destiny?" Jackson asked, pointing to himself and trying to sound smooth. "I'm Jackson. I haven't seen you around here."

"I'm Olivia. I go to school back east. I'm here looking for something fun to do." She flashed Jackson another big smile.

"Well, look no further," Jackson said. "Mr Fun gets off in ten minutes."

"Sounds great," Olivia said. "I'll just go and pack up my stuff." She ran off to the beach.

Jackson couldn't believe his good luck. Could this be real? Beautiful girls usually only thought he was funny in his dreams.

He slapped himself across the face. "Yes! I'm awake," he said.

Cooper ran past Olivia on his way to Rico's. He knew Jackson was about to get off work. "Hey, my brother from another mother, what's cracking?" he asked Jackson.

Jackson hopped over the counter. "Coop, I just hooked up with this amazing girl who was totally into me and I didn't have to tell her that I owned a Ferrari or only had six months to live or any of the usual stuff."

"That's my dawg," Cooper said. "Putting it down for the ladies." He and Jackson shared their secret handshake.

"You should've seen me," Jackson bragged. "And tonight, she's going to find out even my moves have moves." Jackson demonstrated with a totally dorky dance.

Cooper watched with a look of horror on

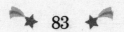

his face. People shouldn't have to look at that, he thought. "Dude, don't do that in public."

Jackson stopped, but he wasn't upset. Olivia was walking towards him with a huge smile on her face. "Check it out," he said. "There she is."

Cooper turned around and watched Olivia walk towards them. "Whoa!" he shouted.

"You bet, 'whoa'," Jackson said proudly.

But Cooper's tone wasn't proud or happy. It was angry. "No, I meant 'whoa', that's my little sister, fool," he snapped.

Jackson gulped. Olivia was Cooper's sister? "I meant 'whoa', I didn't know."

Olivia noticed her brother Cooper talking to her new friend and made a U-turn, but she couldn't get away fast enough.

"Olivia!" Cooper yelled.

Olivia turned around. "Yes, big brother?" she asked sweetly.

"Get over here," Cooper ordered. "Did you agree to go out with this guy?" he asked, pointing at Jackson.

Olivia pretended to be outraged. "Is that what he said?" She turned to Jackson and waggled her finger at him. "Shame on you. What kind of girl do you think I am?" She ducked behind Cooper and peeked around his shoulder to wave and smile at Jackson.

Jackson's forehead wrinkled in confusion. Was this girl trapped in her body along with an evil twin? She said one thing and then sent totally different signals. "But I thought–" Jackson said.

Cooper cut him off. He didn't want to hear it. "Oh, I know what you thought," he snapped, with his arms crossed over his chest. "And you'd better stop thinking it about my little sister."

"Mmm-hmm," Olivia agreed. "Because when my big brother thinks I should stay away from somebody, I stay away," she said, her voice sugary and sweet.

"Mmm-hmm," Cooper agreed. He grabbed Olivia by the arm and stalked away. He didn't notice when his sweet little sister turned around and blew a flirty kiss in Jackson's direction as they left the beach.

Jackson scratched his head. Cooper's sister sure was confusing.

Chapter Four

The next day, Miley, Lilly and Oliver were hanging out on Miley's porch playing cards. Miley put a big bowl of crisps on the table and filled her friends in on her date with Josh. She still couldn't believe that he didn't like Hannah. "This is so frustrating," she said. "I spent all day yesterday trying to get Josh to like Hannah Montana."

"How'd it go?" Oliver asked, fanning out his cards.

Miley pasted a big smile on her face and faked excitement. "It went really well. He loves Hannah now and we're getting married." Then her voice turned sarcastic. "How do you think it went, ya doughnut!"

"I'm going to go with not so well." Oliver looked for a pair. He didn't have one.

"Ding, ding, ding! And we have a winner!" Lilly teased.

"Lilly, I'm serious," Miley said, putting down her cards. "How can I go out with a guy who doesn't like half of me?"

Lilly didn't see the problem. Josh was totally cute and a ninth grader – so what if he didn't like Hannah Montana? "He doesn't know he doesn't like half of you. So just let him think that the half of you he likes is all of you," she reasoned. "As long as the other half keeps her mouth shut, the three of you should make a beautiful couple."

Oliver was completely confused. "I'll never get chick maths," he said, shaking his head.

Miley latched on to Lilly's reasoning. It was that or stop dating Josh and he was too cute to give up. "She's right," Miley nodded. "Why should I have to give Josh up?"

"Yeah," Lilly agreed. "It's not like he's ever going to be in the same place with you *and* Hannah."

But Josh had been thinking about Miley all day, especially about how important Hannah Montana was to her. He didn't get it, but he liked Miley and he wanted to show her that her opinions were important to him. He stopped by to share his big surprise. He knew it would make her really happy.

"Hey, Miley," he said, running up the

porch steps. "You know what you said about Hannah Montana? I decided to give her a chance."

Miley jumped to her feet. "Really? That's great!"

"Yeah, so tonight I'm taking you to her concert," Josh announced with a smile.

"Really? That's . . ." Miley's face froze in a terrified smile while she searched for a response. ". . . even greater," she finally said. She gave Josh a big hug and pretended to be thrilled, but over his shoulder she turned to her friends with a silent plea. "Help!" she mouthed. How could she go to a Hannah Montana concert? She *was* Hannah!

Oliver leaned in and whispered to Lilly. "She thought it didn't go well. Who's the doughnut now?"

"Still you," Lilly said.

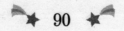

＊ ＊ ＊

Miley and Lilly couldn't think of one convincing excuse that would allow Miley to get out of going to the concert with Josh. Miley wouldn't even consider letting Josh know that she was Hannah Montana. She wanted Josh to like her for who she was, not because she was famous. Plus, what if Josh told someone? Miley knew she could trust Lilly and Oliver with her secret. As much as she liked Josh, she had to admit she didn't know him all that well – yet.

Miley and Lilly spent all afternoon working on a plan. How could Miley keep her date with Josh *and* give a great concert? She couldn't be in two places at once. Or could she?

That night, as Miley and Josh walked into the arena, Miley hoped that the plan she

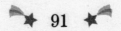

and Lilly had come up with would work. The sold-out crowd was chanting "Hannah! Hannah! Hannah!" A lot of them waved signs with messages for her. "Wow," Miley said, taking in the scene. "So this is what an actual Hannah Montana concert looks like."

"You mean you've never been to one?" Josh asked, puzzled.

Miley had come across to Josh as Hannah's number-one fan, so of course he would think that she had been to lots of Hannah's concerts. "I've tried," Miley said awkwardly. "But somehow I was always busy doing something else."

"Well, tonight, this is all you have to do," Josh said with a smile. He took Miley's hand and led her to their seats.

Miley's heart started to beat a little faster. "You know, I was really nervous when you asked me. But I'm totally glad I said yes."

"Me too," Josh answered. He sat and looked at the crowd. "I just hope she's not one of those divas who keeps everyone waiting. I totally hate that."

"Me too," Miley answered. It was time for her plan to kick in. "I'm going to get a soft pretzel," she said, jumping up.

The two people sitting behind them held their concert programmes in front of their faces. They seemed to be completely engrossed. Miley leaned over them. "You're on," she whispered, so Josh wouldn't hear.

Lilly and Oliver lowered their programmes and pretended to be surprised when they saw that Josh was sitting right in front of them. "Oh, my gosh," Lilly said. "It's Josh. What a coincidence."

"So, what do you think of Hannah Montana so far?" Oliver asked.

Josh's forehead wrinkled in confusion. "She hasn't come on yet."

"Oh, right," Oliver said. "I'm supposed to ask you that later."

Lilly hit Oliver with her programme and shot him a warning look. At this rate, Oliver would give away their whole plan before Miley even came onstage!

Miley raced backstage. She was about to slip into her dressing room when she saw her father come out of it, obviously looking for her. She ducked behind a crate until she could sneak into her dressing room without being spotted.

"Have you seen Hannah?" Mr Stewart asked the stage manager.

"Not since the sound check," he answered.

Mr Stewart checked his watch. It wasn't

like Miley to disappear when she was due onstage. She didn't like to keep her fans waiting. "She's on in a minute. Where is that girl?" he asked.

Miley sneaked into her dressing room and transformed herself into Hannah. All it took was a long blonde wig and her Hannah clothes. Moments later, she rushed out and almost ran right into her father. He was wearing his disguise, too – a big moustache, a wig and a cowboy hat.

"Did you just come out of the dressing room?" Mr Stewart asked.

"Yeah," Miley said.

"I was just in there and you weren't there."

"Yeah, I was," Miley pretended. "You're losing it, Daddy." She rushed off to the stage and her cheering fans.

Robby Stewart shook his head. He was

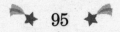

sure Miley hadn't been in that dressing room a minute ago. "Do you think I'm losing it, Fred?" he asked the stage manager.

"I'm Jimmy," the stage manager answered.

"You *are* losing it," Mr Stewart said to himself. At times like these one of his old Tennessee expressions always seemed to fit the bill. "Call the cows home, Robby Ray," he said to himself.

Onstage, Hannah grabbed the microphone. "Hi, everybody," she called to the crowd. "Sorry I'm late. Hope nobody thinks I'm a diva." She was greeted with chants and applause. Her fans were the best, she thought. But what was Josh thinking? Could she turn him into a Hannah fan by the end of the concert?

Chapter Five

At home, Jackson plopped down on the sofa, put his feet up on the coffee table and picked up the phone. Cooper had ruined his plans with the lovely Olivia, so it looked as if he was dateless and home alone on a Saturday night. Again. He decided to order a pizza.

"That's right. Sausage, pepperoni and, what the heck, onions," he said into the phone. "I'm not kissing anybody tonight."

The person taking his order seemed to think that Jackson wouldn't be kissing anybody ever.

"No, I'm not ugly," Jackson said, outraged. Then he tried to prove his point with a lie. "I'm a six-foot-four beach god," he pretended.

He hung up the phone and heard a musical knock on the door.

"Jackson? It's me, Olivia. Open up!" she sang.

"Olivia?" Jackson couldn't believe she was there. He ran his hands through his hair and almost knocked over a vase while grabbing a flower. He rubbed it on his neck for aftershave and under his armpits for deodorant. He shook off his nervousness and struck a macho pose before opening the door. "Hi," he said.

"Olivia's here," she said, striking her own

pose. "And it's time to get our Saturday night on!"

Jackson's head was spinning. Did this girl have a split personality or something? "I don't understand," he said. "You were totally different today with Cooper."

"Well, that was Saturday afternoon," Olivia said with a smile. "The moon has come up, and I am coming out." She threw her arms up into the air. "I heard there's a party over here!"

"Who said that?" Jackson asked, following her.

"Me. Just now." Olivia flicked on the stereo and danced into the kitchen. "Come on, boy, keep up." She spotted a snack. "Ooh, buttered popcorn." She popped it into the microwave and started to dance.

Jackson was still confused. His best

buddy Coop had made it very clear – Jackson was supposed to stay away from Olivia. And Olivia had agreed. But now here she was, dancing in Jackson's kitchen. "Cooper's not going to be too happy that you're here," Jackson said.

"I know. That's why I didn't tell him." She took Jackson by the hand and led him to the phone. "Now let's get you on the phone and let's people this party."

Jackson was still confused. Was she going to turn back into the Olivia from this afternoon, or was the party girl here to stay? "What happened to all that 'when my big brother says stay away, I stay away. Mmm-hmm'?" he asked, imitating her high voice.

Olivia rolled her eyes. "Oh, Cooper thinks I'm a sweet little girl who needs to be protected," she said with a shrug. "And what he doesn't know won't hurt him."

They were interrupted by a knock on the door. "Jackson, it's Coop."

Jackson froze. Cooper would flip if he found Olivia there. "Yeah, but it might hurt me. You've got to go," Jackson told her.

"No way," Olivia said. "This is my last night in town, and I'm not going to let it be spoiled by Cooper the party pooper." Olivia pushed Jackson towards the door. "I'll hide. You get rid of him."

Jackson sighed. He had a little sister of his own. He understood how Cooper felt about Olivia and Cooper was a good friend. "I don't know," Jackson said. "I've never lied to him before."

Olivia turned on the charm. "Please?" She kissed her fingertips and then placed them on Jackson's lips. "For me?" She giggled and flirted.

Jackson was won over. How could he say no? "Well, there's a first time for everything." He pointed to the side door leading to the porch. "You wait out there."

"Okay." Olivia ran outside.

"C'mon in, Coop," Jackson yelled as soon as Olivia was outside. Suddenly, he panicked. Would Cooper want to know why Jackson was listening to dance music? Jackson launched into a bizarre combination of Irish clogging and hip-hop. "Just getting my Saturday night on," Jackson said, in response to Cooper's raised eyebrows.

Cooper watched with a look of horror on his face. Jackson was his best friend, but Cooper had to admit, the boy could not dance. "Well, get it off before you hurt yourself," he said.

Jackson turned the music off. All he could think about was Olivia hiding on the porch, waiting for him. He had to get rid of Cooper and fast. "That's a good idea," Jackson babbled. "That's some great advice. Thanks for stopping by. Give me a call when you make it home so I know that you're safe."

Cooper was ready to apologize. "Look, man, I know I came down hard on you and I just want to make sure we're cool," he said.

"We are totally cool. Drive safe. See you tomorrow." Jackson tried to lead his friend to the door.

Cooper wouldn't be rushed. It was Saturday night. He and Jackson always hung out on Saturday nights. "Slow down," he said. "I rented a few DVDs. Thought we could chill."

The microwave beeped. Cooper sniffed the air. "Mmm – buttered popcorn?" He tapped Jackson on the shoulder with a knowing smile. "You knew I was coming all along."

"Believe me," Jackson said, watching his friend head to the kitchen and get ready to hang out for a while, "I had no idea."

Olivia stuck her head through the door and waved, flashing Jackson a huge smile. He followed Cooper into the kitchen, trying to think of ways to get his best friend to leave before he found his sister hiding on the porch.

Chapter Six

Onstage, Miley finished her opening number. Her fans waved their hands in the air and cheered, asking for more. She usually loved giving them what they wanted, but right now she had to get back to Josh.

"Thank you! And now, give it up for the fabulous fingers of Jesse Jay, lead guitar." Miley rushed offstage, past Jimmy and Mr Stewart.

"Whoa, whoa, whoa," her father said. "Where are you going?"

Miley's eyes darted around, looking for an excuse. Then she came up with one. She clutched her stomach and doubled over. "Nervous stomach," she said with a grimace. She ran towards her dressing room. "Could be a while."

Robby Stewart shook his head and headed back to the stage. Miley was acting awfully strange tonight, he thought.

Seconds later, Miley sneaked out of her dressing room. She had taken off her Hannah wig and slipped back into her Miley clothes. She grabbed a soft pretzel out of Jimmy's hand and yelled thanks over her shoulder as she ran back to her seat and Josh.

Oliver was playing air guitar along with Jesse Jay while Lilly danced in her seat.

Hannah's fans were starting to wonder what had happened to her. And Josh was starting to wonder what had happened to his date. The only reason he came to the concert was to spend time with Miley and she had completely disappeared.

"This is the longest guitar solo ever," Josh said.

"I know. He rocks!" Lilly said. She noticed that Oliver was going overboard with his enthusiasm. They were supposed to help Josh see how great Hannah Montana was, but no one liked guitar solos *that* much. "Sit down!" she hissed to Oliver, so Josh wouldn't hear.

A breathless Miley rushed in and dropped into her seat. "You wouldn't believe the queue for soft pretzels," she said. But what she really wanted to know was whether Josh was warming up to

Hannah. "So how about that first song? Pretty awesome, huh?" she prodded.

"It was okay," Josh said.

"Okay?" Miley asked. "Not even really okay?"

Josh shrugged. "I guess I'm just more into hip-hop."

"Hip-hop?" Miley asked. There wasn't anything close to hip-hop on her song list.

"Yeah, does she ever do that?" Josh asked.

"I have a feeling she will *tonight*," Miley answered with a smile. If Josh wanted hip-hop, Miley would find a way. How hard could it be? Josh had to leave this concert loving Hannah Montana. He just had to. But first Miley had to get back onstage.

Lilly was ready and waiting with Miley's excuse. They had worked it all out that afternoon. "Is that pretzel making you thirsty?" Lilly asked. "Do you need to go and get a drink?"

"You know what? I do!" Miley jumped to her feet, ready to run.

But Oliver was still caught up in the guitar solo and forgot all about their plan. He tried to hand Miley his drink. "Wait," he said. "You can have some of mine."

Miley froze. What should she do now? Lilly knocked Oliver's drink out of his hand. "Whoops," she said. "I'm sorry. My fault."

Josh was watching the three of them with a totally bewildered expression.

Miley had to cover. She turned to him with a big smile. "I'm having so much fun with you, Josh. Bye!" Then she raced off again.

Moments later, the longest guitar solo in history ended when Miley took the stage as

Hannah. She launched into a hip-hop number right away. The problem was, she didn't have a hip-hop number and had to make it up as she went along. Her band had given up trying to follow her, so it was just Miley and her voice. She waved her hands in the air as she rapped.

I bet you didn't know
that this girl could really go
and I'm gonna give you mo'
'cause you spent a lotta dough
a-comin' to the show
doe-dee-doe-dee-doe-dee-doe!
Word!

The audience gaped at her in complete shock. Josh was totally disgusted. This was the worst hip-hop number he had ever heard and that included the six-year-old rapper at his little sister's first-grade talent show.

Miley tried to get the audience involved. She waved her hands in the air. "Hey . . . ho!" she sang. "Say hey . . . ho!"

Oliver and Lilly jumped to their feet and joined in. "Hey ho, hey ho." Lilly grabbed Josh's arms and tried to get him to join in, too, but he wasn't the only one who didn't love Miley's attempts at hip-hop. The rest of her fans watched in stunned confusion. The cheering stopped. What had happened to their Hannah Montana?

Chapter Seven

Back at the house, Jackson and Cooper watched a DVD. Cooper was engrossed, but Jackson had other things on his mind, namely the beautiful girl hiding on the porch! What would Cooper do if he spotted her there?

Jackson sneaked a peek at her. Olivia pointed to her watch and motioned for Jackson to get rid of her brother.

"Man," Jackson said, coughing, "I think I'm coming down with something."

Cooper moved over. "Well, keep it away from me."

"I'll try," he said. Jackson leaned in Cooper's direction and coughed harder – all over Cooper and all over the popcorn. "Better?" he asked.

Cooper stood. "I'm getting out of here before you cough up an alien."

"That's a good idea," Jackson said, coughing. "Better safe than sorry."

"And listen," Cooper said. "About my sister . . ."

"Hey," Jackson stopped him. "Not another word. Please." Jackson felt guilty enough already. He didn't want Cooper to apologize again and make him feel worse.

"I know I'm a little overprotective," Cooper explained. "But I just care about her a lot. And I appreciate you backing off. You're a good friend."

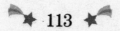

Jackson's shoulders slumped as he watched his buddy leave. Yeah, a really good friend, he thought. How could he do this to Cooper?

Olivia came in, rubbing her arms. "I thought he'd never leave. It's freezing out there. But nothing a good party can't warm up." She turned the music back on and tried to pull Jackson into a dance.

Jackson turned off the music. He couldn't believe he was about to send a beautiful girl away, but his friendship with Cooper was too important. It was the only thing he could do. "Okay, hold on," Jackson said. "Didn't you hear your brother? I'm a good friend. And good friends do not party with their friends' sisters, no matter how much they want to."

"Wow, you really are a nice guy. Just my luck," Olivia said, sounding disappointed.

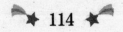

"And you really have to go," Jackson said, sounding even more disappointed. "Just *my* luck." He led Olivia to the front door.

"Well, I guess this is goodbye." Olivia flashed a beautiful smile and held out her hand for a handshake. "Nice meeting you."

Jackson took her hand. "You, too."

Olivia pulled him into a kiss just as the door opened.

"Hey, I forgot my DVD," Cooper said. Then he saw Olivia and Jackson kissing. "Dang!" he yelled.

Olivia pushed Jackson away and pretended to be upset. "I just came over to say goodbye and he was all over me," she said to Cooper. "You are in truhhhh-ble," she said to Jackson.

Cooper glared at him, too angry to speak.

"That is *so* not what happened," Jackson said to Cooper.

"Olivia, you wait in the car," Cooper ordered.

"Yes, big brother," Olivia said in a syrupy-sweet voice. She turned to Jackson again and frowned. "Shame on you."

Jackson tried to explain. "She's not telling you the truth. She came over here. She was all over me. I swear, Coop."

Cooper threw his hands up in the air. "Save it. I can't believe you're trying to blame my sweet, innocent little sister for this."

"I'm telling you, she's not sweet and innocent!"

"Okay, you know what? That's enough! If there's one thing I know about my sister, it's that she would never be *all over* any guy she just met." Cooper opened the door to join Olivia in the car, but she was still on the porch. And now she was kissing the pizza-delivery guy!

"Pizza's here," Jackson said, dryly.

Olivia's eyes widened. She tried to use the same excuse again. "He was all over me?" she said, as if it was a question.

Cooper shook his head. He couldn't believe it! Jackson was telling the truth. His little sister wasn't so sweet and innocent after all. "Get in the car, Olivia. You and I are going to have a little talk."

"Mmm-hmm!" Jackson and Cooper said as they shared their secret handshake.

Cooper glared at the pizza-delivery guy and handed the pizza to Jackson before setting off after his sister.

The delivery guy held his hand out for a tip. Jackson shook his hand instead. "She already gave you your tip, big boy," he said.

Chapter Eight

Back at the concert, Miley had changed out of her Hannah clothes – again! – and rushed back to her seat. Josh was starting to get annoyed. He had come to the concert to be with Miley and she was spending all her time queuing for pretzels and pop.

"Where've you been?" he asked. "You're missing the whole concert."

"That drinks queue went on forever,"

Miley said.

Oliver sipped a new drink. "No it didn't. There were, like, three people in it."

Lilly rolled her eyes. Oliver kept forgetting their plan. "Then you won't mind going to get another one," she said through clenched teeth. Once again, she knocked his drink onto the floor.

"Oh, man!" Oliver said, heading back to the drinks queue.

Miley turned to Josh with a smile. She couldn't wait to find out if her hip-hop number had swayed him at all. The rest of her fans didn't love it, but maybe Josh did. "So what do you think of Hannah Montana now?" she asked.

Josh shrugged. He was a little bored. "I'm still not feeling it."

"What do you want her to do, surf

the crowd?" Lilly asked.

Josh's face brightened. "Yeah, that'd be cool!"

Miley glared at Lilly. Now she was the one speaking through clenched teeth. "Surf the crowd," she said sarcastically. "Then I guess I have to get another pretzel." Miley ran off, stopping only to knock the drink out of Lilly's hand.

Minutes later, dressed as Hannah, Miley was surfing the crowd. She worried about crashing to the floor and losing her wig as her fans passed her around the arena. She tried to convince herself that she was actually enjoying this.

"Having fun surfing!" she said. "Please don't drop me! Please don't–" She was passed to Lilly and Oliver and suddenly noticed that Josh's seat was empty. "Where'd he go?" she asked.

"He left," Lilly told her.

"What?" Miley asked sadly.

"I'm sorry," Lilly said, as Miley was passed deeper into the crowd.

Miley finally made it back to the stage and finished her concert. She gave a great performance, as always, but her heart wasn't in it. Afterwards, back in her Miley clothes and without her Hannah wig, she sat next to Oliver and Lilly in the empty arena.

"He said it was the worst date of his life?" Miley asked, repeating Lilly's last words.

"I'm sorry," Lilly said. She knew her friend was hurting, but she didn't know how to make her feel better.

"Didn't he say anything else?" Miley asked.

"He also said that Hannah Montana stinks, but we decided to leave that out. I mean, why hurt you any more than you already are?" Oliver said sympathetically.

Lilly loved Oliver, but when it came to making his friends feel better, he could be totally clueless. She turned to him with a steely stare. "Leave. Now."

Oliver started to leave, but he wanted to say something nice first to cheer up Miley. "The rap was . . ." he searched for a word, ". . . interesting."

Lilly pointed to the door. "Go!" she ordered.

Miley turned to her best friend. "I cannot believe I just blew it."

"You didn't blow it," Lilly said gently.

But Miley knew she had. Josh would never ask her out again. "Yes, I did. I couldn't be happy with a cute guy liking just me. I tried to make him like Hannah, too and now he hates both of us."

Mr Stewart came in behind them. "Well, as far as I'm concerned, that's his loss," he said. "But I'm butting in. I'm sure Lilly was just getting ready to say that."

"Yeah," Lilly agreed. Mr Stewart had made a good point, but Lilly didn't know what else to say. "What was I going to say next?" she asked.

"That someday she'll find a guy that likes everything about her. There won't be anything to change," he said.

Miley smiled sweetly at Lilly. "Thanks, Lilly," she said, loud enough for her father to hear. "You always know what to say."

Lilly grinned back. "Sometimes it just comes to me."

"Come on, girls," Mr Stewart said, standing. "It's time to go . . ."

They started to leave the arena, but Mr Stewart couldn't resist teasing Miley just a little bit about that night's performance. ". . . 'cause it's the end of the show and we're walkin' out the do' and we're headin' for the big, black stretch limo."

Miley stopped him before it got any worse. "Dad! Remember? You ain't funny."

"And you can't rap," he said, throwing his arm around her with a smile.